To:_____

From:_____

**Carl Brenders,** born in Belgium and educated at art schools in his native country, is one of the world's most accomplished nature painters. He is a four-time recipient of the "Award of Excellence," given by the Society of Animal Artists in New York, and has won the National Tour People's Choice Award. Many of Brenders's paintings have been published as limited edition art prints.

# SONG *of* CREATION

## ART BY
## CARL BRENDERS

 Baker Books

A Division of Baker Book House Co
Grand Rapids, Michigan 49516

© 2000 by Baker Book House

Art copyright by Carl Brenders by arrangement with Mill Pond Press.

Published by Baker Books
a division of Baker Book House Company
P.O. Box 6287, Grand Rapids, MI 49516-6287

Printed in the United States of America

All rights reserved. No part of this publication may be reproduced, dismantled or framed, stored in a retrieval system, or transmitted in any form or by any means—for example, electronic, photocopy, recording—without the prior written permission of the publisher. The only exception is brief quotations in printed reviews.

ISBN 0-8010-1198-1

Scripture is taken from the King James Version of the Bible.

For information about art prints by Carl Brenders call Mill Pond Press, 800-535-0331.

Cover and interior design by Robin K. Black.

# Contents

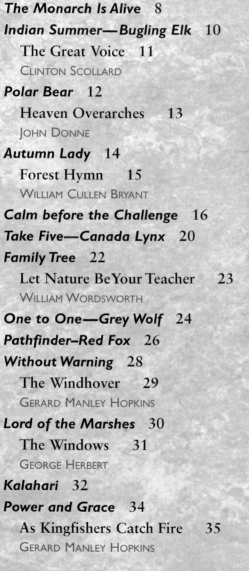

*But they that wait upon the LORD shall renew their strength: they shall mount up with wings as eagles; they shall run, and not be weary; and they shall walk, and not faint.*

ISAIAH 40:31

# The Great Voice

I who have heard solemnities of sound—
The throbbing pulse of cities, the loud roar
Of ocean on sheer ledges of gaunt rock,
The chanting of innumerable winds
Around white peaks, the plunge of cataracts,
The whelm of avalanches, and, by night,
The thunder's panic breath—have come to know
What is earth's mightiest voice—the desert's voice—
Silence, that speaks with deafening tones of God.

CLINTON SCOLLARD, 1860–1932

# Heaven
# Overarches

Heaven overarches earth and sea,
   Earth-sadness and sea-bitterness.
Heaven overarches you and me:
A little while and we shall be—
Please God—where there is no more sea
   Nor barren wilderness.

Heaven overarches you and me,
   And all earth's gardens and her graves.
Look up with me, until we see
The day break and the shadows flee:
What though tonight wrecks you and me
   If so tomorrow saves?

*JOHN DONNE, 1572–1631*

# Forest Hymn

The groves were God's first temples. Ere man learned
To hew the shaft, and lay the architrave,
And spread the roof above them,—ere he framed
The lofty vault, to gather and roll back
The sound of anthems; in the darkling wood,
Amidst the cool and silence, he knelt down
And offered to the Mightiest, solemn thanks
And supplication. For his simple heart
Might not resist the sacred influences,
Which, from the stilly twilight of the place,
And from the gray old trunks that high in heaven
Mingled their mossy boughs, and from the sound
Of the invisible breath that swayed at once
All their green tops, stole over him, and bowed
His spirit with the thought of boundless power
And inaccessible majesty. Ah, why
Should we, in the world's riper years, neglect
God's ancient sanctuaries, and adore
Only among the crowd, and under roofs
That our frail hands have raised? Let me, at least,
Here, in the shadow of this aged wood,
Offer one hymn—thrice happy, if it find
Acceptance in his ear.

*(continued on page 17)*

Father, thy hand
Hath reared these venerable columns, thou
Didst weave this verdant roof. Thou didst look down
Upon the naked earth, and, forthwith, rose
All these fair ranks of trees. They, in thy sun,
Budded, and shook their green leaves in thy breeze,
And shot toward heaven. The century-living crow,
Whose birth was in their tops, grew old and died
Among their branches, till, at last, they stood,
As now they stand, massy, and tall, and dark,
Fit shrine for humble worshipper to hold
Communion with his Maker. These dim vaults,
These winding isles, of human pomp or pride
Report not. No fantastic carvings show,
The boast of our vain race to change the form
Of thy fair works. But thou art here—thou fill'st
The solitude. Thou art in the soft winds,
That run along the summit of these trees
In music;—thou art in the cooler breath,
That from the inmost darkness of the place,
Comes, scarcely felt;—the barky trunks, the ground,
The fresh moist ground, are all instinct with thee.

*(continued on page 18)*

Here is continual worship;—nature, here,
In the tranquillity that thou dost love,
Enjoys thy presence. Noiselessly, around,
From perch to perch, the solitary bird
Passes; and yon clear spring, that, 'midst its herbs,
Wells softly forth and visits the strong roots
Of half the mighty forest, tells no tale
Of all the good it does. Thou hast not left
Thyself without a witness, in these shades,
Of thy perfections. Grandeur, strength, and grace
Are here to speak of thee. This mighty oak—
by whose inmovable stem I stand and seem
Almost annihilated—not a prince,
In all that proud old world beyond the deep,
E'er wore his crown as loftily as he
Wears the green coronal of leaves with which
Thy hand has graced him. Nestled at his root
Is beauty, such as blooms not in the glare
Of the broad sun. That delicate forest flower,
With scented breath, and look so like a smile,
Seems, as it issues from the shapeless mould,
An emanation of the indwelling Life,
A visible token of the upholding Love,
That are the soul of this wide universe.

My heart is awed within me, when I think
Of the great miracle that still goes on,
In silence, round me—the perpetual work
Of thy creation, finished, yet renewed
Forever. Written on thy works I read
The lesson of thy own eternity.
Lo! all grow old and die—but see, again,
How on the faltering footsteps of decay
Youth presses—ever gay and beautiful youth
In all its beautiful forms. These lofty trees
Wave not less proudly that their ancestors
Moulder beneath them. Oh, there is not lost
One of earth's charms: upon her bosom yet,
After the flight of untold centuries,
The freshness of her far beginning lies
And yet shall lie. Life mocks the idle hate
Of his arch enemy Death—yea, seats himself
Upon the tyrant's throne—the sepulchre,
And of the triumphs of his ghastly foe
Makes his own nourishment. For he came forth
From thine own bosom, and shall have no end.

*(continued on page 21)*

There have been holy men who hid themselves
Deep in the woody wilderness, and gave
Their lives to thought and prayer, till they out-lived
The generation born with them, nor seemed
Less aged than the hoary trees and rocks
Around them;—and there have been holy men
Who deemed it were not well to pass life thus.
But let me often to these solitudes
Retire, and in thy presence reassure
My feeble virtue. Here its enemies,
The passions, at thy plainer footsteps shrink
And tremble and are still. Oh, God! when thou
Dost scare the world with tempests, set on fire
The heavens with falling thunderbolts, or fill,
With all the waters of the firmament,
The swift dark whirlwind that uproots the woods
And drowns the villages; when, at thy call,
Uprises the great deep and throws himself
Upon the continent, and overwhelms
Its cities—who forgets not, at the sight
Of these tremendous tokens of thy power,
His pride, and lays his strifes and follies by?
Oh, from these sterner aspects of thy face
Spare me and mine, nor let us need the wrath
Of the mad unchained elements to teach
Who rules them. Be it ours to meditate
In these calm shades thy milder majesty,
And to the beautiful order of thy works,
Learn to conform the order of our lives.

WILLIAM CULLEN BRYANT, 1794–1878

# Let Nature Be Your Teacher

*From "The Tables Turned"*

And hark! how blithe the throstle sings!
He, too, is no mean preacher:
Come forth into the light of things,
Let Nature be your teacher.

She has a world of ready wealth,
Our minds and hearts to bless—
Spontaneous wisdom breathed by health,
Truth breathed by cheerfulness.

One impulse from a vernal wood
May teach you more of man,
Of moral evil and of good,
Than all the sages can.

*(continued on page 25)*

Sweet is the lore which Nature brings;
Our meddling intellect
Mis-shapes the beauteous forms of things:—
We murder to dissect.

Enough of Science and of Art;
Close up those barren leaves;
Come forth, and bring with you a heart
That watches and receives.

WILLIAM WORDSWORTH, 1770–1850

# A Christian must exercise goodness toward every living creature.

JOHN WOOLMAN (1720–1772)

27

# The Windhover

## *To Christ Our Lord*

I caught this morning morning's minion, kingdom of daylight's
   dauphin, dapple-dawn-drawn Falcon, in his riding
   Of the rolling level underneath him steady air, and striding
High there, how he rung upon on the rein of a wimpling wing
In his ecstasy! then off, off forth on swing,
   As a skate's heel sweeps smooth on a bow-bend: the hurl
    and gliding
   Rebuffed the big wind. My heart in hiding
Stirred for a bird—the achieve of, the mastery of the thing!

Brute beauty and valour and act, oh, air, pride, plume here
   Buckle! AND the first that breaks from thee then, a billion
Times told lovelier, more dangerous, O my chevalier!
   No wonder of it: sheer plod makes plough down sillion
Shine, and blue-bleak embers, ah my dear,
   Fall, gall themselves, and gash gold-vermilion.

GERARD MANLEY HOPKINS, 1844–1889

29

# The Windows

Lord, how can man preach thy eternal Word?
 He is a brittle, crazy glass;
Yet in thy temple thou dost him afford
 This glorious and transcendent place,
 To be a window, through thy grace.

But when thou dost anneal in glass thy story,
 Making thy life to shine within
The holy preachers, then the light and glory
 More reverend grows, and more doth win,
 Which else shows waterish, bleak, and thin.

Doctrine and life, colors and light, in one
 When they combine and mingle, bring
A strong regard and awe; but speech alone
 Doth vanish like a flaring thing,
 And in ear, not conscience, ring.

*GEORGE HERBERT, 1593–1633*

31

The wicked flee when no man pursueth: but the righteous are bold as a lion.

PROVERBS 28:1

# As Kingfishers Catch Fire

As kingfishers catch fire, dragonflies draw flame;
As tumbled over rim in roundy wells
Stones ring; like each tucked string tells, each hung bell's
Bow swung finds tongue to fling out broad its name;
Each mortal thing does one thing and the same:
Deals out that being indoors each one dwells;
Selves—goes itself; myself it speaks and spells;
Crying What I do is me: for that I came.

I say more: the just man justices;
Keeps grace: that keeps all his goings graces;
Acts in God's eye what in God's eye he is—
Christ, for Christ plays in ten thousand places,
Lovely in limbs, and lovely in eyes not His
To the Father through the features of men's faces.

*GERARD MANLEY HOPKINS, 1844–1889*

# The Starlight Night

Look at the stars! look, look up at the skies!
O look at all the fire-folk sitting in the air!
The bright boroughs, the circle-citadels there!
Down in dim woods the diamond delves! the elves'-eyes!
The gray lawns cold where gold, where quickgold lies!
Wind-beat whitebeam! airy abeles set on a flare!
Flake-doves sent floating forth at a farmyard scare!
Ah, well! it is all a purchase, all is a prize.
Buy then! bid then!—What?—Prayer, patience, alms, vows.
Look, look: a May-mess, like on orchard boughs!
Look! March-bloom, like on mealed-with-yellow sallows!
These are indeed the barn; withindoors house
The shocks. This piece-bright paling shuts the spouse
Christ home, Christ and His mother and all His hallows.

GERARD MANLEY HOPKINS, 1844–1889

We are beginning to regain a knowledge of creation, a knowledge forfeited by the fall of Adam. By God's mercy we can begin to recognize His wonderful works and wonders also in flowers when we ponder his might and goodness. Therefore we laud, magnify and thank him.

MARTIN LUTHER (1483–1546)

# All Things Bright and Beautiful

All things bright and beautiful,
　All creatures great and small,
All things wise and wonderful,
　The Lord God made them all.

Each little flower that opens,
　Each little bird that sings,
He made their glowing colours,
　He made their tiny wings.

The purple-headed mountain,
　The river running by,
The sunset and the morning
　That brighten up the sky,

The cold wind in the winter,
　The pleasant summer sun,
The ripe fruits in the garden,
　He made them, every one.

*(continued on page 43)*

The tall trees in the greenwood,
  The meadows where we play,
The rushes by the water,
  We gather every day.

He gave us eyes to see them,
  And lips that we might tell
How great is God Almighty,
  Who has made all things well.

CECIL FRANCES ALEXANDER, 1818–1895

# Ode

The spacious firmament on high,
With all the blue ethereal sky,
And spangled heavens, a shining frame,
Their great Original proclaim.
The unwearied sun, from day to day,
Does his Creator's power display,
And publishes to every land
The work of an Almighty hand.

Soon as the evening shades prevail,
The moon takes up the wondrous tale,
And nightly to the listening earth
Repeats the story of her birth;
Whilst all the stars that round her burn,
And all the planets in their turn,
Confirm the tidings as they roll,
And spread the truth from pole to pole.

What though in solemn silence all
Move round the dark terrestrial ball;
What though no real voice or sound
Amidst their radiant orbs be found:
In reason's ear they all rejoice,
And utter forth a glorious voice,
Forever singing as they shine,
"The hand that made us is divine."

JOSEPH ADDISON, 1672–1719

45

# These Are
# Thy Glorious Works

## *From "Paradise Lost," Book V*

These are thy glorious works, Parent of good,
Almighty! thine this universal frame,
Thus wondrous fair! Thyself how wondrous then!
Unspeakable! who sitt'st above these Heavens
To us invisible, or dimly seen
In these thy lowest works; yet these declare
Thy goodness beyond thought and power divine.

*JOHN MILTON, 1608–1674*

*While we contemplate in all creatures, as in a mirror, those immense riches of his wisdom, justice, goodness and power, we should not merely run them over cursorily, and, so to speak, with a fleeting glance, but we should ponder them at length, turn them over in our mind seriously and faithfully, and recollect them repeatedly.*

JOHN CALVIN (1509–1564)

The wolf also shall dwell with the lamb, . . . and the calf and the young lion and the fatling together; and a little child shall lead them.

ISAIAH 11:6

# One World

## From "The Divine Comedy"

I raised my eyes aloft, and I beheld
The scattered chapters of the Universe
Gathered and bound into a single book
By the austere and tender hand of God.

DANTE ALIGHIERI, 1265–1321

# The Glory of God in Creation

Thou art, O God, the life and light
    Of all this wondrous world we see;
Its glow by day, its smile by night,
    Are but reflections caught from Thee.
Where'er we turn, Thy glories shine,
And all things fair and bright are Thine!

When day, with farewell beam, delays
    Among the opening clouds of even,
And we can almost think we gaze
    Through golden vistas into heaven—
Those hues that make the sun's decline
So soft, so radiant, Lord! are Thine.

When night, with wings of starry gloom,
    O'ershadows all the earth and skies,
Like some dark, beauteous bird, whose plume
    Is sparkling with unnumber'd eyes—
That sacred gloom, those fires divine,
So grand, so countless, Lord! are Thine.

When youthful Spring around us breathes,
    Thy Spirit warms her fragrant sigh;
And every flower the Summer wreathes
    Is born beneath Thy kindling eye:
Where'er we turn, Thy glories shine,
And all things fair and bright are Thine!

*THOMAS MOORE, 1779–1852*

55

**God** is wholly present in all creation, in every corner, behind you and before you. Do you think God is sleeping on a pillow in heaven? God is watching over you and protecting you.

MARTIN LUTHER (1483–1546)

# God of the Earth, the Sky, the Sea

God of the earth, the sky, the sea,
Maker of all above, below,
Creation lives and moves in Thee;
Thy present life through all doth flow.

Thy love is in the sun-shine's glow,
Thy life is in the quickening air;
When lightnings flash and storm winds blow,
There is Thy power, Thy law is there.

We feel Thy calm at evening's hour,
Thy grandeur in the march of night,
And when the morning breaks in power,
We hear Thy word, "Let there be light."

But higher far, and far more clear,
Thee in man's spirit we behold,
Thine image and Thyself are there,—
Th' in-dwelling God, proclaimed of old.

SAMUEL LONGFELLOW, 1819–1892

# Design

This is a piece too fair
To be the child of Chance, and not of Care.
No Atoms casually together hurl'd
Could e'er produce so beautifull a world.

JOHN DRYDEN, 1631–1700

# Inscription
# for the Entrance
# to a Wood

    Stranger, if thou hast learned a truth which needs
No school of long experience, that the world
Is full of guilt and misery, and hast seen
Enough of all its sorrows, crimes, and cares,
To tire thee of it, enter this wild wood
And views the haunts of Nature. The calm shade
Shall bring a kindred calm, and the sweet breeze
That makes the green leaves dance, shall waft a balm
To thy sick heart. Thou wilt find nothing here
Of all that pained thee in the haunts of men
And made thee loathe thy life. The primal curse
Fell, it is true, upon the unsinning earth,
But not in vengeance. God hath yoked to Guilt
Her pale tormentor, Misery. Hence, these shades
Are still the abodes of gladness; the thick roof
Of green and stirring branches is alive
And musical with birds, that sing and sport
In wantonness of spirit; while below
The squirrel, with raised paws and form erect,
Chirps merrily. Throngs of insects in the shade
Try their thin wings and dance in warm beam
That waked them into life. Even the green trees
Partake the deep contentment; as they bend

To the soft winds, the sun from the blue sky
Looks in and sheds a blessing on the scene.
Scarce less the cleft-born wild-flower seems to enjoy
Existence, than the winged plunderer
That sucks its sweets. The massy rocks themselves,
And the old and ponderous trunks of prostrate trees
That lead from knoll to knoll a causey rude
Or bridge the sunken brook, and their dark roots,
With all their earth upon them, twisting high,
Breathed fixed tranquillity. The rivulet
Sends forth glad sounds, and trippling o'er its bed
Of pebbly sands, or leaping down the rocks,
Seems, with continuous laughter, to rejoice
In its own being. Softly tread the marge,
Lest from their midway perch thou scare the wren
That dips her bill in water. The cool wind,
That stirs the stream in play, shall come to thee,
Like one that loves thee nor will let thee pass
Ungreeted, and shall give its light embrace.

WILLIAM CULLEN BRYANT, 1794–1878

The creation is quite like a spacious and splendid house, provided and filled with the most exquisite and at the same time the most abundant furnishings. Everything in it tells of God.

JOHN CALVIN (1509–1564)

# The Storm

If the winds and waters here below
    Do fly and flow,
My sighs and tears as busy were above,
    Sure they would move
And much affect Thee, as tempestuous times
Amaze poor mortals, and object their crimes.

Stars have their storms, ev'n in a high degree
    As well as we.
A throbbing conscience spurred by remorse
    Hath a strange force;
It quits the earth, and mounting more and more,
Dares to assault Thee and besiege Thy door.

There it stands knocking, to Thy music's wrong,
    And drowns the song.
Glory and honor are set by, till it
    An answer get.
Poets have wronged poor storms: such days are best;
They purge the air without, within the breast.

*GEORGE HERBERT, 1593–1633*

*Some people, in order to discover God, read books. But there is a great book: the very appearance of created things. Look above you! Look below you! Note it. Read it. God, whom you want to discover, never wrote that book with ink. Instead He set before your eyes the things that He had made. Can you ask for a louder voice than that?*

*God writes the Gospel, not in the Bible alone, but also on trees,*
*and in the flowers and clouds and stars.*

MARTIN LUTHER (1483–1546)

# To a Waterfowl

Whither, 'midst falling dew,
While glow the heavens with the last steps of day,
Far, through their rosy depths, dost thou pursue
Thy solitary way!

Vainly the fowler's eye
Might mark thy distant flight to do thee wrong,
As, darkly painted on the crimson sky,
Thy figure floats along.

Seek'st thou the plashy brink
Of weedy lake, or marge of river wide,
Or where the rocking billows rise and sink
On the chafed ocean side?

There is a Power whose care
Teaches thy way along that pathless coast,
The desert and illimitable air—
Lone wandering, but not lost.

All day thy wings have fanned,
At that far height, the cold thin atmosphere,
Yet stoop not, weary, to the welcome land,
Though the dark night is near,

And soon that toil shall end;
Soon shalt thou find a summer home, and rest,
And scream among thy fellows; reeds shall bend,
  Soon, o'er thy sheltered nest.

  Thou'rt gone, the abyss of heaven
Hath swallowed up thy form; yet, on my heart
Deeply hath sunk the lesson thou hast given,
  And shall not soon depart.

  He who, from zone to zone,
Guides through the boundless sky thy certain flight,
In the long way that I must tread alone
  Will lead my steps aright.

WILLIAM CULLEN BRYANT, 1794–1878

# The Gladness of Nature

Is this a time to be cloudy and sad,
　　When our mother Nature laughs around;
When even the deep blue heavens look glad,
　　And gladness breathes from the blossoming ground?

There are notes of joy from the hang-bird and wren,
　　And the gossip of swallows through all the sky;
The ground-squirrel gayly chirps by his den,
　　And the wilding bee hums merrily by.

The clouds are at play in the azure space,
　　And their shadows at play on the bright green vale,
And here they stretch to the frolic chase,
　　And there they roll on the easy gale.

There's a dance of leaves in that aspen bower,
There's a titter of winds in that beechen tree,
There's a smile on the fruit, and a smile on the flower,
　　And a laugh from the brook that runs to the sea.

And look at the broad-faced sun, how he smiles
　　On the dewy earth that smiles in his ray,
On the leaping waters and gay young isles;
　　Ay, look, and he'll smile thy gloom away.

WILLIAM CULLEN BRYANT, 1794–1878

# Why Are We
# By All Creatures?

Why are we by all creatures waited on?
Why do the prodigal elements supply
Life and food to me, being more pure than I,
Simple and further from corruption?
Why brookest thou, ignorant horse, subjection?
Why dost thou, bull and boar, so sillily
Dissemble weakness, and by one man's stroke die,
Whose whole kind you might swallow and
    feed upon?
Weaker I am, woe is me, and worse than you;
You have not sinned, nor need be timorous.
But wonder at a greater wonder, for to us
Created nature doth these things subdue,
But their Creator, whom sin nor
    nature tied,
For us, His creatures, and His foes,
    hath died.

JOHN DONNE, 1572–1631